Ethnic Albanians Need Not Apply

A CHEAPCAFFEINE COLLECTION

NATHAN SHUMATE
and diverse hands

Published by

COLD FUSION MEDIA

www.coldfusionmedia.us
www.cheapcaffeine.net

Cold Fusion Media
http://www.coldfusionmedia.us

CheapCaffeine
http://www.cheapcaffeine.net

Introduction

Because this is why you picked up a book of cartoons, right? So you could read a page of text first?

In answer to the question most occasioned by the contents of this collection: Yes, I *can* draw. However, in order to produce a daily webcomic along with holding down a normal job and engaging in any number of other pursuits (eating, sleeping, etc.), I chose instead to use pre-existing artwork, of which there are inconceivable mountains, just waiting to be rescued from obscurity into slightly lesser obscurity.

This webcomic was begun under two sources of inspiration: *Wondermark.com* by David Malki, which similarly uses public domain illustrations, and *Treelobsters.com* by some guy named Steve, whose full identity is apparently a closely guarded secret (or at least doesn't reveal itself to a fair bit of Googling). If you don't like what you see, you can split the blame evenly between them.

The great thing about the internet is that there is that anything can have fans, even subjects or content which the overwhelming majority of sentient beings find to be offensive, distasteful, or simply unworthy of their attention. It is to that 00.01% of the internet that I dedicate the current volume.

A Note About Sources

A fair amount of the clipart used in these cartoons comes from two sources:

openclipart.org
www.clker.com

Both of these sites are venues for users to post clipart which they have either created originally or extracted and converted from material no longer under copyright. My thanks to these tireless gleaners of the past.

I have also relied heavily on ClipArt ETC, found at *etc.usf.edu/clipart*. The license agreement at that page stresses that these images are to be used for educational purposes, which is why (I think you'll agree) I have gone out of my way to make these comics just as enlightening and edifying as they are funny. The more you know!

But most importantly, I am indebted to the tireless volunteers of Project Gutenberg, who have digitized thousands of old publications, complete with illustrations. (I have found their archives of the old British publication Punch to be especially helpful.) A Google image search on *gutenberg.org* has yielded not only many of the images that I have sought in order to render a specific cartoon concept, but many serendipitous images that I have saved into my "resources" folder for future use.

#1 Intimacy

Because there's no better way to begin a webcomic than with a groin rash.

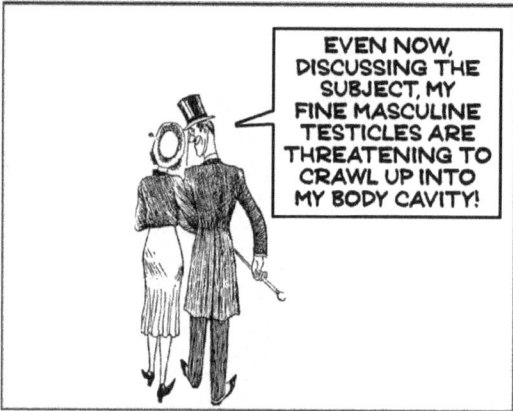

#2 Duties of Affection

#3 Stage Behavior

So I have a bunch of these characters in a couple of "dingbat" fonts, and I thought I'd end up making frequent use of them in the comic. To date, I believe this is the only time they've shown up.

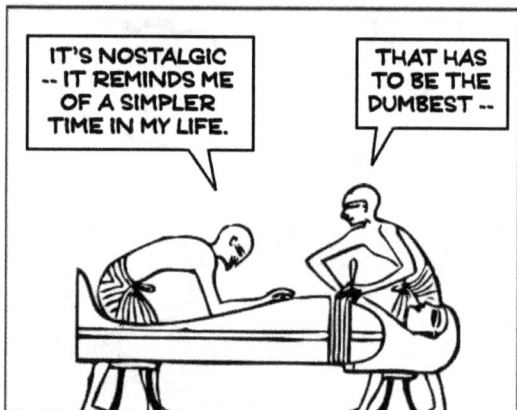

#4 Voices of the Past

This is a PSA from the American Board of Health.

"Have you educated yourself on the risk to your family of **nebulon gas exposure** in your home?"

"Nebulon is a naturally occurring contaminant which can cause debilitating illness in small amounts. it is not geographically confined; anyone, anywhere, could be exposed."

"Not only is nebulon invisible and odorless, it cannot be detected by any test known to medical science."

"Your only option is to endure in a state of perpetual dread and anxiety.

Thank you and goodnight."

#5 A Public Service Announcement

#6 Living in the Past

#7 Rules of Engagement

#8 How One's Heart is Set

The introduction of what went on to be a continuing character. Who can predict such things? Who, indeed?

#9 Eternal Spamnation

On the off-chance that you're interested: This one underwent considerable refinement for this book, all concentrated on the last panel. The person originally used there a) wasn't Egyptian at all, thus conflicting with the art motif of the first three panels, and b) also appeared in some of those one-panel "e-cards" that you see bandied around Facebook with a political quip. Hey, it's public domain, but I didn't want it to be *that* public!

#10 The Contents of One's Stocking

#11 Band Loyalty

No particular band in mind here, though I'm sure you can fill in "The Squashmonkeys" with any number of acts in your own music collection.

#12 Lyricism

#13 Steadfast Resolve

#14 Hold the Pickle

#15 Commerce

And thus, from a random bit of nonsense, a running gag commences.

#16 Intimations of Mortality

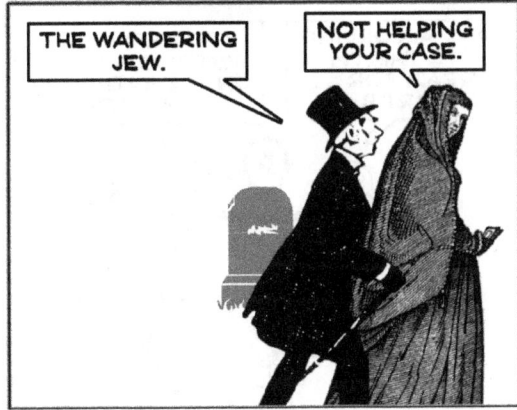

#17 Age Ain't Nothing But Some Years

#18 Hurdles of Romance

Why yes, I *do* intend to be that kind of father in just a few years.

#19 A Comparison

So far, my sole experiment in truncating or otherwise varying the standard four-panel format of the strip. (It was actually a gag I sketched on a scrap of paper at least fifteen years ago; using it in CheapCaffeine, however much it varied from the normal format of the strip, at least allowed me to throw away that unfileable scrap of paper.)

However, I feel uncomfortable leaving you with all this space on the page, so here's a picture of a steampunk snail. ***Bonus content!!1!***

#20 Goals

This was, of course, during what I call "The Twinkie-Less Interregnum." No one knew if Hostess snack foods would ever come back, or worse, if the nefarious powers that be would take this cessation in production as an occasion to forever alter the time-honored recipe, much as the Coca-Cola Company had done with "Coke Classic," exchanging cane sugar for high-fructose syrup.

What dark times those were.

#21 Refrain

By the way, the politician's speech is cribbed from Calvin Coolidge's 1925 inaugural address. But I'm sure a well-educated person such as yourself already knew that.

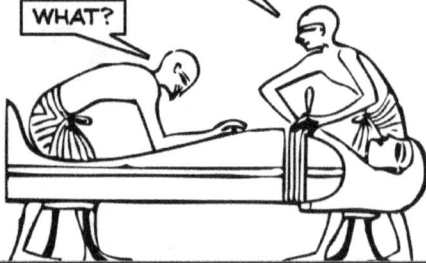
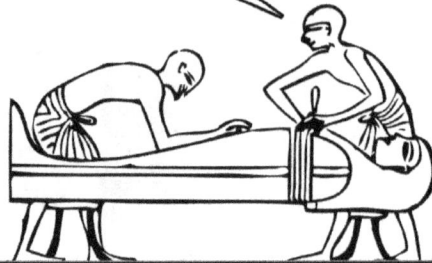
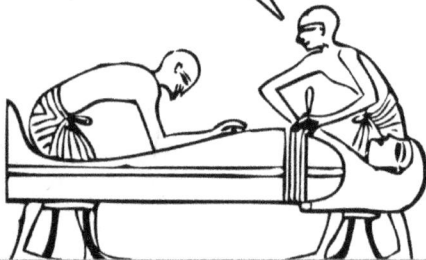
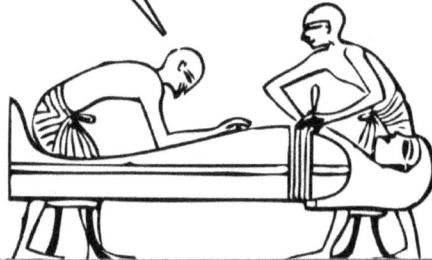

#22 Limits

#23 Unaccustomed to Her Face

As with many of the cartoons herein, the first panel of this one is autobiographical. The rest, not so much.

#24 A Science is a Science is a Science

#25 Hurdles Revisited

#26 Extinction

#27 The Social Machine

#28 Be Your Guide

#29 The Whole World Smiles With You

#30 The Siege Mentality

#31 Luncheon

After I posted this, I found out that Woody Allen had used the same punchline fully forty years before in the movie *Sleeper* (1973), a movie which I saw twenty-five years ago. Maybe that gag had lingered in my subconscious, even after my conscious mind forgot it. Or maybe at some point in the future, Woody Allen will take advantage of a newly invented time machine and take a copy of this book back to his younger self to plagiarize shamelessly. I'm not convinced either way.

#32 Intractable

#33 The Identity Triptych, Part I

#34 The Identity Triptych, Part II

#35 The Identity Triptych, Part III

#36 Appendectology

#37 Through a Glass, Darkly

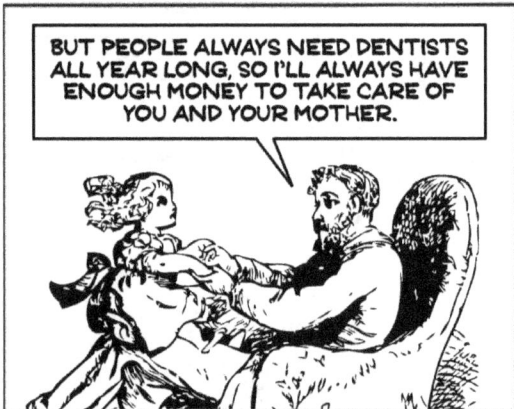

#38 Careerism

#39 Self-Diagnosis

Ask your doctor if anti-mutation gene therapy treatment is right for you.

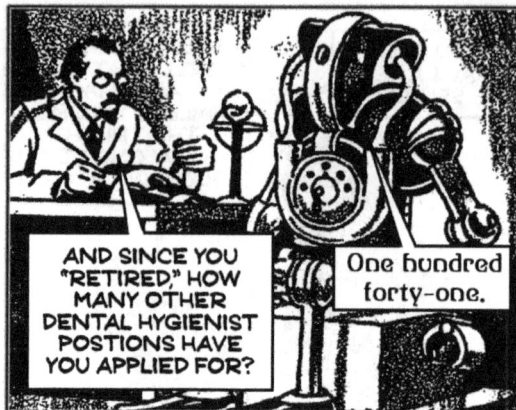

#40 Skill Sets

#41 Where One's Hat is Hung

#42 Substitute Goals

#43 Energy

#44 Upon Which the Sun Never Sets

#45 Protestations of Love

#46 Dietary Context

Note: As originally posted, I had relied entirely on my memory for the spelling of several words which turned out to be inaccurate. A reader who identified himself as a medical professional took my to task for my original misspellings of "atherosclerosis" and "pellagra." Those errors are herein corrected.

He also pointed out the inaccuracy of saying that too much corn *causes* pellagra (which is a disease of vitamin deficiency), but hey, if you're trusting the medical information you get from a talking cup of diet soda...

#47 Hierarchy of Light

#48 Parity

#49 An In-Joke

#50 Scrapage

#51 Verbiage

#52 Hackery

Far too autobiographical, I'm afraid.

#53 A Parable

#54 A Crackshot

#55 Barriers

#56 Franchisation

In making this strip, I created a full-color version of the *Hobbit IV* poster here, sure that someone would want to see it—maybe even order a print of it.

Nobody asked.

Sigh...

#57 Franchisation: The Sequel

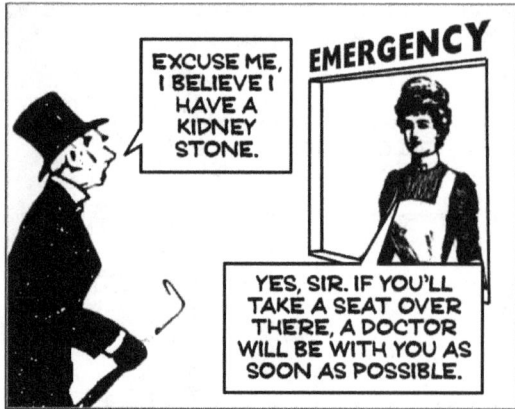

#58 Patience

Again, far too autobiographical.

#59 Disgorgement

#60 Pizzaesque

All completely factual.

#61 The Immigrant's Story

#62 Genealogy

Not that there's anything wrong with that.

#63 Transit

#64 Flowchart

#65 The Meat of the Matter

#66 The Lack of the Irish

#67 Celtageddon

#68 Appreciation

#69 Strategy

#70 Consolation

#71 Influences

And then an astute reader pointed out that the creator of Wondermark is *David* Malki, not John.

Rather than correct the mistake, though, I used it for a springboard for another strip.

(And now this becomes a choose-your-own-adventure book: "If you want to see how the mistake was corrected, turn to strip #118. If you want to continue reading, go to strip #72.")

#72 That Which We Call

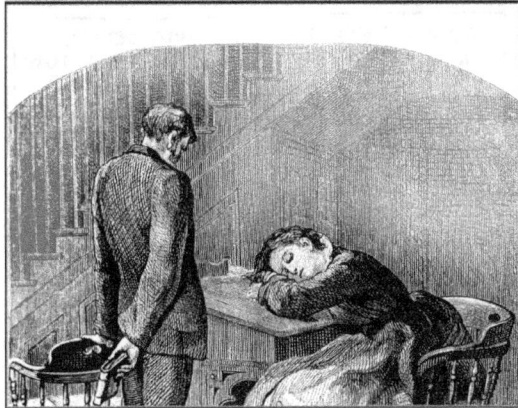

#73 Impulse Control

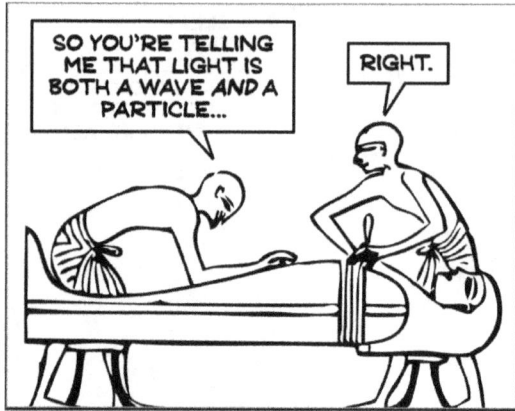

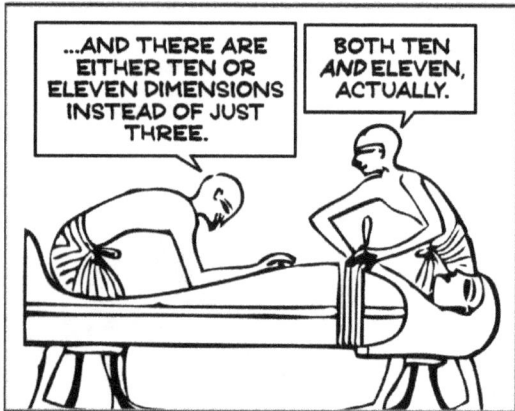

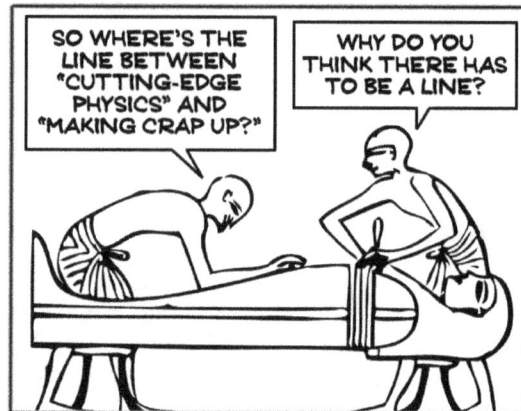

#74 Reality

Note: The first two panels are accepted scientific principles. The third, not so much. (I'm not saying that that isn't how reality is, I'm just saying that no one has suggested it in a peer-reviewed venue.)

#75 Neoteny

#76 Winning Features

#77 Strange Bedfellows

#78 Just Irony

#79 Libraridolatry

#80 Why We Vacation Separately

Whenever I have wanted to prove the insipidity of American pop-culture and those who eagerly consume it, I always use *Mr. Belvedere* as my example. The usual formulation is, "*Max Headroom* only lasted fourteen episodes, but *Mr. Belvedere* ran for six seasons!" (You can replace "*Mad Headroom*" with "*Firefly*," if you so choose.)

#81 All Politics is Local Politics

#82 Timelessness

#83 Apotheosis

Because whenever you can make a cheap *Monty Python* reference, go for it.

#84 Pinchability

#85 The Heart Which Is Hidden

#86 Unmediated Communication

#87 The Rich Are Different

#88 April

Note: This comic never appeared online. I had obviously meant for it to go up in April, but April 2013 saw a massive server breakdown at my then-webhost—and wouldn't you know it, but those daily backups they touted as being part of their service? Yeah, they weren't exactly doing them. So after over two weeks of getting the runaround from these hosting monkeys, I began rebuilding CheapCaffeine.net on another host—and by that time, it was May and the window for this comic had passed.

So that means—***bonus content!!!1!***

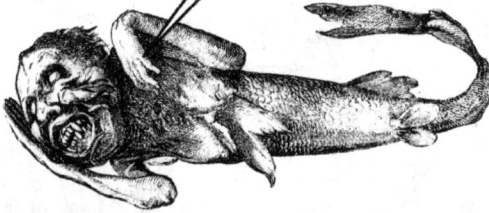

This is the FeeJee Mermaid.

'SUP.

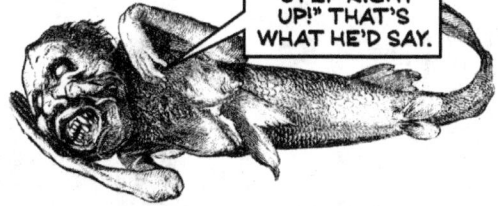

Exhibited by P.T. Barnum from 1842 until the late 1860s, the FeeJee Mermaid was supposedly the carcass of a female "sea-human."

"STEP RIGHT UP!" THAT'S WHAT HE'D SAY.

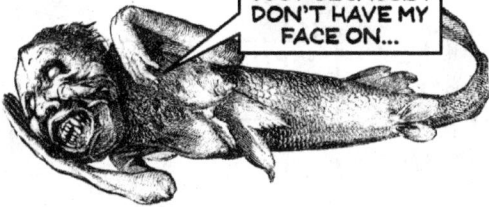

Although Barnum advertised the exhibit with woodcuts of traditionally beautiful (and topless) mermaids, the reality was somewhat less alluring.

JUST BECAUSE I DON'T HAVE MY FACE ON...

One assumes that seamen were looking through "grog-goggles."

HEY, SAILOR! YOO-HOO!

#89 FeeJee, FeeJeer, FeeJeest

#90 The Mad Science Generation Gap

#91 Mutation Nation

#92 Speaking of the Future

Isn't it great living in a more enlightened age?

#93 Blurring the Distinction

#94 The Ladder to Success

#95 The Root Cause

#96 Interactivity

#97 The Long Dark Stream of Consciousness of the Soul

#98 The Sticking Point

#99 Paranoid Circumlocutions

#100 So It Shall Be Written

#101 Balance and Ballast

#102 That Hidden Aura

#103 Romance Hurdled

#104 A Gastronomical Wager

And now, as a public service, CheapCaffeine.net provides an overview of the various Twinkie substitutes in the absence of the authentic article. We call it...

THE LEGION OF SUBSTITUTE TWINKIES

"Golden Creme Cakes" by Great Value (the Walmart house brand): Possibly the first fake Twinkies on the scene, because Walmart's just that canny. A very delectable snack cake, although it's missing something indefinable in the flavor of a true Twinkie.

"Cloud Cakes" by Little Debbie: Roughly as good as the Great Value version, but the slight inauthenticity herein is different than the one exhibited by Great Value. What is this secret ingredient? Is it the joy and laughter of children? One of the Colonel's secret herbs and spices? Something the Joker stole?

"Golden Creme Cakes" by Mrs. Freshley's: Although a fine snack in its own right, it tastes more of cake mix and disappoints those searching for a true Twinkie substitute. On a sidenote, if you're planning on a career in baked goods, "Freshley" is a much more fortunate surname than "Bitters" or "O'Putrid."

"Submarinos" by Merinela: The very torments of Hell on Earth. These taste like Satan used them as ▓▓▓▓▓ in his ▓▓▓▓▓. It is fervently hoped that you have no enemies so hated that you would wish these upon them.

I HOPE YOU CAN JOIN WITH ME IN SUPPLICATING WHATEVER GODLIKE ENTITIES YOU WORSHIP FOR A SPEEDY RETURN OF THE TRUE TWINKIE, EMBLEM OF ALL THAT IS GOOD AND NOBLE IN THIS TERRESTRIAL AGE OF WONDERS.

UNTIL THEN, KEEP WATCHING THE SKIES!

#105 The Legion of Substitute Twinkies

It was, as I said, a dark dark time.

#106 Held Precious

#107 Germane to the Discussion

Confession: When I made this comic, I had completely forgotten that I had used the same illustration as the basis for comic #97, which is why they don't relate to or build upon each other at all.

#108 Ahead of the Capitalism Curve

#109 Sic Transit

#110 Pre-Histamines

I know, being averse to physical trauma isn't the same thing as "allergic," but I doubt that two Egyptian morticians are well informed about allergens.

CheapCaffeine Presents

THE FEEJEE MERMAID MEETS THE GRIEVANCE GORILLA

THE END

#111 An Epic in Two Panels

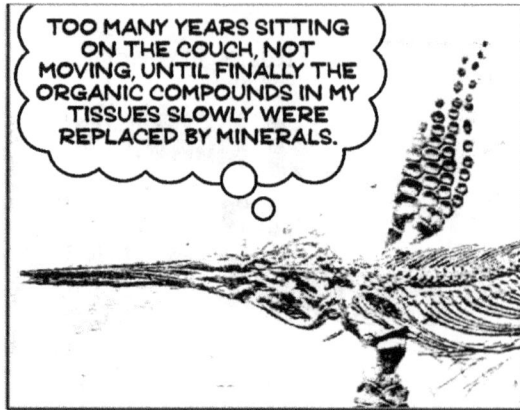

#112 Petrification

#113 The Aggregate Army

#114 How the Breakfast Is Made

#115 A Song is What You Make It

Although all of the old lady's sing-along lyrics are based on actual songs, the only lyrical source I can recall is for the last one, which is Def Leppard's "Pour Some Sugar On Me."

#116 Arachnology

Fact: Paul McCartney's mother was indeed named Mary. The line in the first verse of "Let It Be"—*Mother Mary comes to me*—isn't a reference to Catholic tradition, but simply to his mother. Because comics should be educational.

#117 Arachnogeny

#118 Mea Caffeinated Culpa

And now you finally know why the pages are this shape.

#119 Legislative Focus

WAIT -- IT WAS *MY* TURN TO BRING THE FUNNY? AW, CRAP.

#120 Meta-Responsibility

Thanks to such postmodern funnymen as David Letterman, one can sparingly fall back on the "no joke is the joke" trope. Sparingly.

#121 What's in Plato's Wallet?

#122 Family First

#123 Not That There's Anything Wrong With That

#124 That Certain Je Ne Sais Quoi

#125 Culinary Imperatives

#126 Procession

And who's idea was Neopolitan ice cream, anyway? "No matter who you are, your least favorite flavor is in every scoop!"

#127 That Old-Time Music

#128 What It Says on the Box

#129 The Most Important Meal of the Day

Say, I just realized I ran two breakfast cereal-related comics in as many days. It's subtext!

#130 Appearances Must Be Kept

#131 Faster Than a Speeding Critic

#132 Women's Health—Uncovered!

#133 The Rebel Metrics

But is it hipsteriffic? Please don't tell me if it is.

The Mütter Museum, part of the College of Physicians of Philadelphia, is a historical repository of educational medical specimens.

"From a collection originally donated by Dr. Thomas Mütter in 1858, the Mütter Museum is best known for its exhibits of human oddities, injuries and birth defects."

"On display are skeletons, preserved tissues, and wax casts of conjoined twins, deformed limbs, and bizarre facial growths."

"With 178 black and white illustrations and 24 color plates."

All very interesting, but I'm not sure it's really "first date" material.

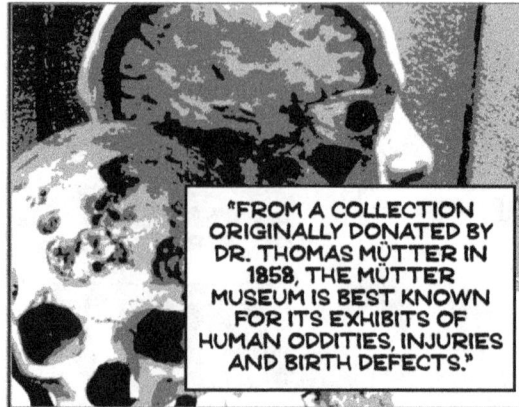

#134 Mütter Nature

If I were to start a webcomic in which I drew by hand all of the panels (which would require a colossal influx of free time so don't hold your breath), odds are the characters would be drawn from the medical oddities of the Mütter Museum.

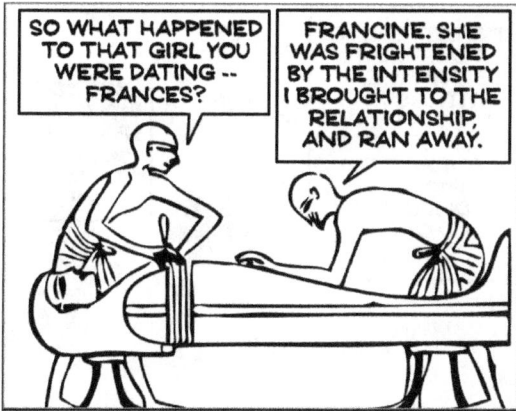

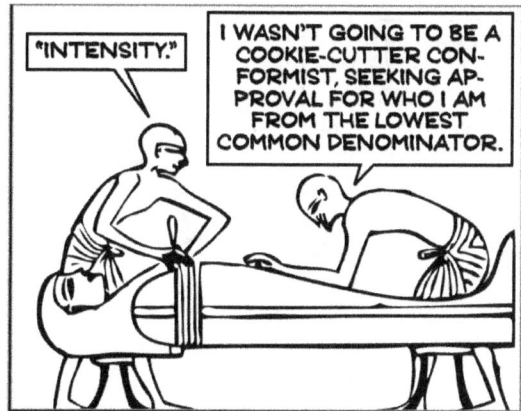

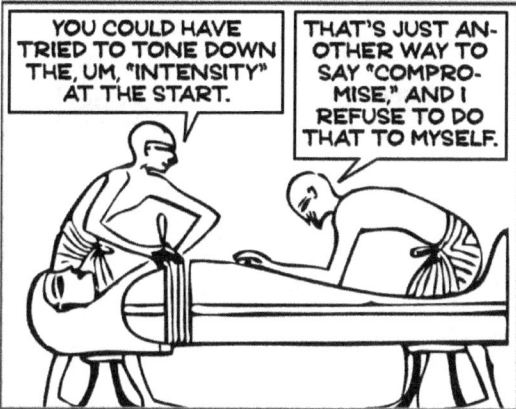

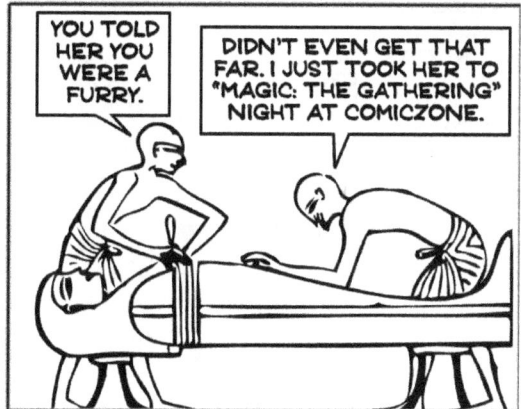

#135 To Thine Own Self Be True

#136 Sister Act

#137 Unpapered

It seems to me that *all* philosophical quandaries should be solved by an appeal to *Star Trek*.

#138 The Honeypot of Capitalism

#139 Vindicating That Old-Time Music

#140 Which Way the Wind Blows

#141 Harbinger

(See what I did there in that title?)

#142 It Comes and It Goes

That being said, I don't drink coffee myself. Diet Dr Pepper (from the fountain, decidedly) is my caffeine delivery medium of choice.

#143 Pearls Before Swine

Autobiographical, naturally.

#144 Your Dreams, Within Reason

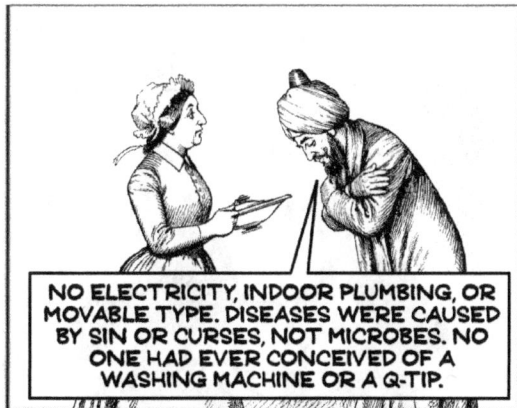

#145 A Miracle in Context

#146 Maybe You DON'T Know Art When You See It

#147 Oh, the Humanity!

#148 Art, Played Out

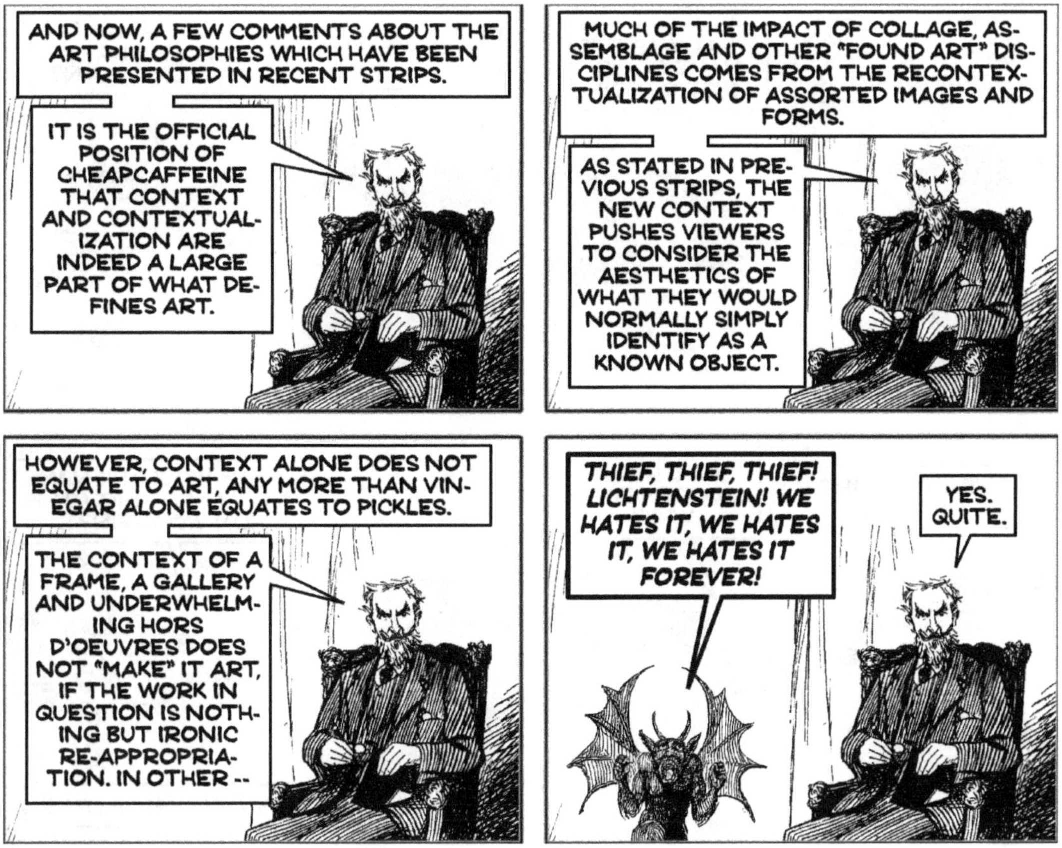

#149 Putting It All in Context

#150 Pull the Other What?

#151 The Fish With Which We Swim

#152 Criminality

#153 Cha-Cha-Cha-Changes

And yet here you are, reading the print version of a comic that first appeared online! Isn't it ironic? Don't you think?

Talking Back to Absolutes

I DON'T WANT TO RULE THE WORLD.

I *ALWAYS* EXPECT THE SPANISH INQUISITION.

I DO NOT HAVE A FACE THAT I HIDE AWAY FOREVER. I THEREFORE DO NOT TAKE IT OUT AND SHOW MYSELF WHEN EVERYONE HAS GONE.

I PUT BABY IN THE CORNER *ALL. THE. TIME.*

#154 Talking Back to Absolutes

#155 Scanning

\#156 Headless Can't Be Choosers

#157 Wakefulness

I WOULD ASSUME THAT SEVERAL OF OUR READERS ARE PUZZLED AT THE LACK OF A STRIP CELEBRATING THE RECENT RETURN OF *THE TWINKIE.*

AFTER ALL, WE AT CHEAPCAFFEINE HAVE USED TWINKIES AND THEIR SUDDEN UNAVAILABILITY AS A RECURRING THEME IN OUR COMICS.

THE RETURN OF THE TWINKIE IS A MOMENTOUS MOMENT IN WESTERN CIVILIZATION, AND THE LABELLING OF SUCH AS *"THE SWEETEST RETURN IN THE HISTORY OF EVER"* IS NOT AT ALL HYPERBOLIC.

FRANKLY, WE ARE HAVING TROUBLE EXPRESSING OUR JUBILATION IN A MANNER WHICH DOES JUSTICE TO THE JOYOUS OCCASION.

OBVIOUSLY, *THE MARTIAN* IS THE MOST APPROPRIATE CHARACTER AMONG THE CHEAPCAFFEINE PLAYERS TO TAKE CENTER STAGE IN SUCH A CELEBRATION.

IT WAS HE WHO, IN HIS FOCUS ON TWINKIES AS THE SOLE REASON TO BOTHER CONQUERING EARTH, TURNED A THROWAWAY PUNCHLINE INTO A RUNNING GAG.

UNFORTUNATELY, THE MARTIAN HAS BEEN IN A SELF-INFLICTED SUGAR COMA SINCE TWINKIES WERE RESTOCKED AT THE LOCAL WALMART.

TURNS OUT THAT MARTIANS ARE DIABETIC. WHO KNEW?

#158 The Twinkie Parousia

#159 I've Seen the Future, Baby, It is Murder

#160 The Bounties of Nature

#161 The Unrefined Truth

#162 Desperate Measures

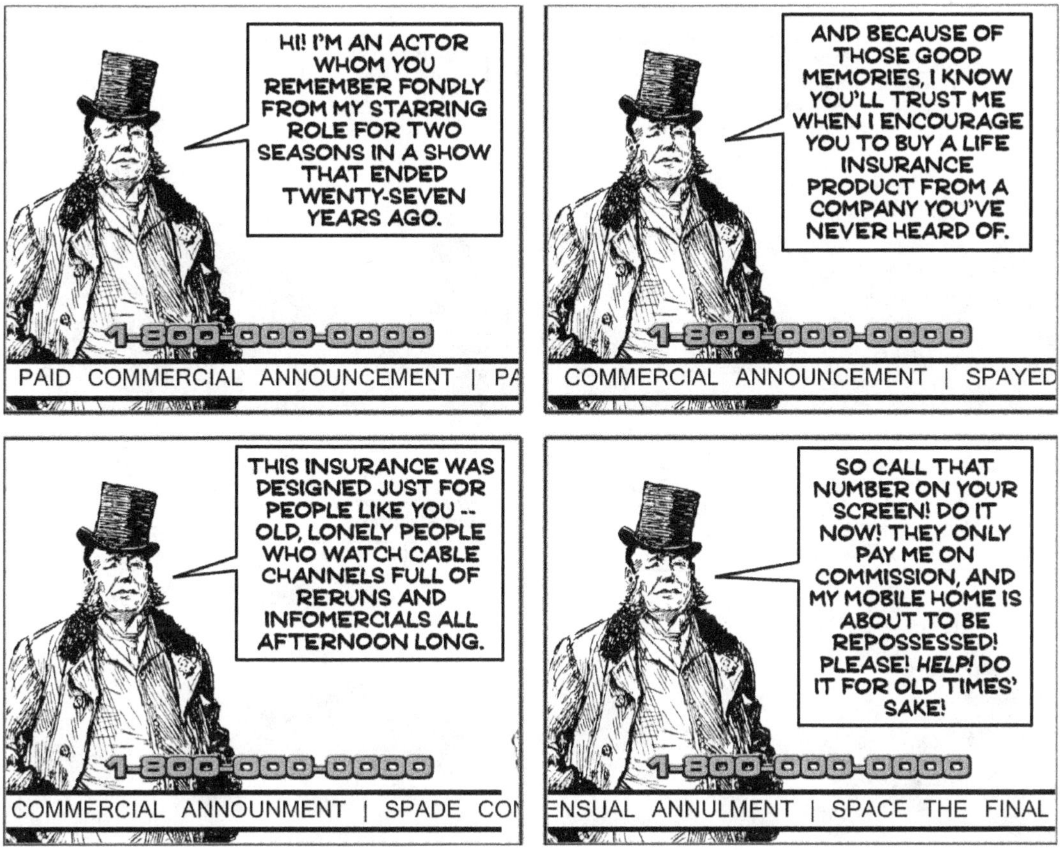

#63 And Now, A Word From Our Sponsors

#164 Schadenfreude

#165 Servitude

#166 Conceptual Fish

Inspired by true events, although the fishy smell wasn't intentional, I swear.
Also, "Conceptual Fish" is the name of my next band.

#167 Primogeniture

Panel 1:
LOOK AT ALL THE LITTLE RUGRATS, RUNNING BACK TO SCHOOL! PRECIOUS, AREN'T THEY?

YES, VERY ENDEARING.

Panel 2:
JUST THINK -- A FEW YEARS AFTER WE'RE MARRIED, *WE* CAN EXPERIENCE THE SAME HAPPINESS!

HAVING CHILDREN, YOU MEAN?

Panel 3:
MORE THAN THAT -- WATCHING THEM *FINALLY* GO BACK TO SCHOOL AFTER A SUMMER AT HOME!

SO YOU'RE LOOKING FORWARD TO CHILDREN SO YOU CAN SIGH WITH RELIEF WHEN THEY LEAVE.

Panel 4:
IT SOUNDS KIND OF SILLY WHEN YOU PUT IT THAT WAY.

DOESN'T IT, THOUGH.

#168 Vacation

Hmm... It appears that, due to some kind of error which completely couldn't have been my fault, this strip never appeared on the website. ***More bonus content!!1!***

#168 The Eternal Question

Or maybe it was some kind of server error that wiped out a few days' worth of comics after the fact. Whatever the reason, you should feel gratified!

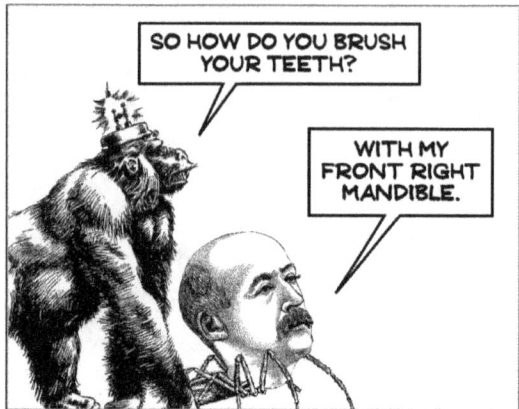

#70 Orthodontal Orthodoxy

#171 The Best of Intentions

#172 The Trump Card, Trumped

#173 Invention is the Mother of Invention

#174 Scraping Bottom

The first Salt Lake Comic Con, held September of 2013, garnered an attendance of well over 100,000 participants—so many that the fire marshal finally forbade further entrants. I had absolutely nothing to do with its success, but that doesn't deter home team spirit. Yay, us!

#175 A Lack of Direction

#176 The Freedom of Dreams

#177 The Hollywood Formula

#178 Whate'er Thou Art

#179 Discontent

#180 Forces of Habit

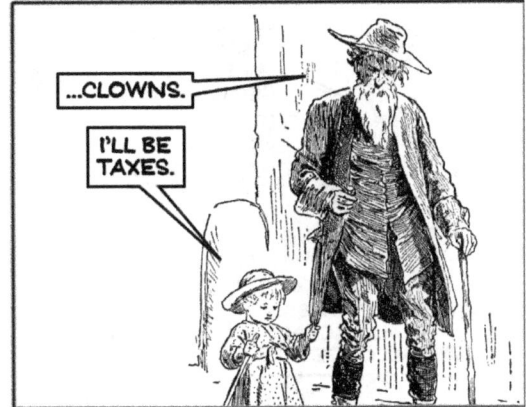

#181 Dread

I swear, the first two panels (three, really) are entirely autobiographical.

#182 Sibilance

#183 References

#184 Patronage

THE MILLION-MAN-MARCH FOR THE RIGHT TO BEAR CLUBS

PRIVACY GUIDELINES FOR THE PONY EXPRESS

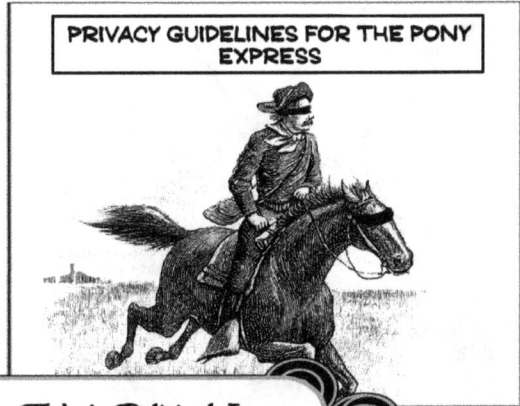

Historical Precedents to Today's Political Issues

SECURITY PATDOWNS ON THE OREGON TRAIL

FREE LEECHES

A SAWBUCK FOR A SAWBONES? I SAY THEE NAY

GOVERNMENT-SPONSORED HEALTHCARE

#185 Precedents

#186 Attraction

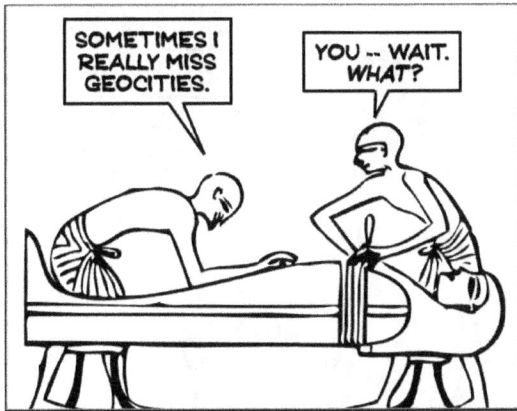

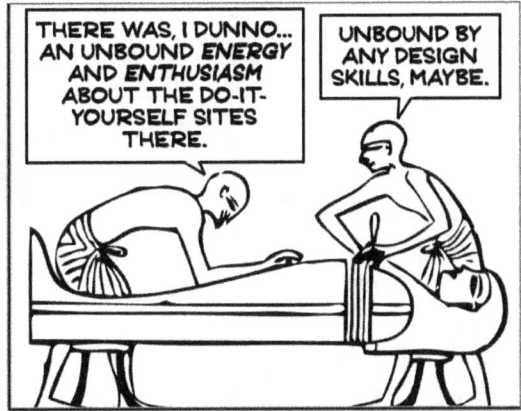

#187 Nostalgia

#188 Education

This grew out of an attempt to persuade one of my children to do his homework. (I wasn't successful.)

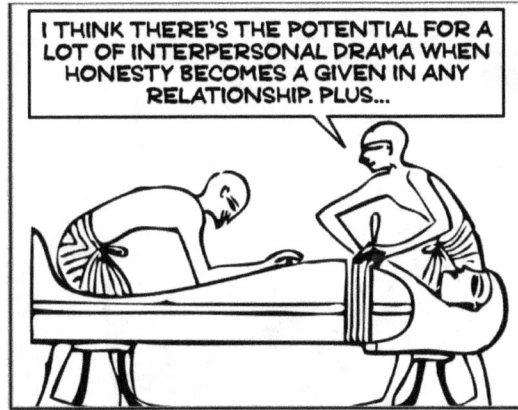

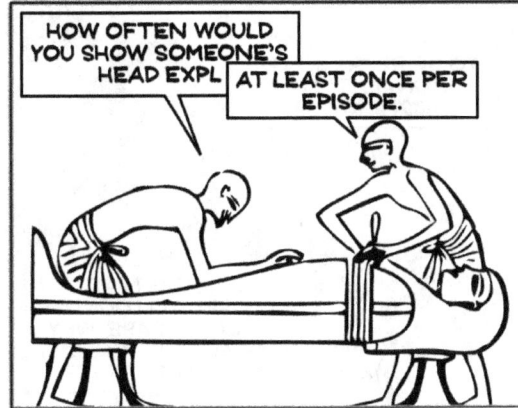

#189 Scanners

Two comics in this collection which reference the *Scanners* movies? Subtext!

#190 The Artist's Eye

#191 Savings

#192 Space

#193 Cold

#194 Quest

#195 Legacy

#196 Even Her Hairdresser Doesn't Know For Sure

AUDITIONING NEW MEMBERS OF THE CHEAPCAFFEINE PLAYERS

I AM CHARLES BIGGLESWORTH III. MY WIFE SUGGESTED I PARTICIPATE MORE IN COMMUNITY THEATER. NOT TO BRAG, BUT I THINK I'M "LEADING MAN" MATERIAL.

I'M THE GLOBE-HEADED MAN! MY HEAD LOOKS LIKE THE EARTH! I CAN ALSO SPIN AROUND!

IT TAKES A FEW HOURS.

I'M THE TRANSPARENT CHICKEN, AND I CAN LAY GLASS-SHELLED EGGS.

I ALSO POOP A LOT. FAIR WARNING.

I'M THE GRIEVANCE GECKO. "LOOK AT ME! I'VE BEEN HISTORICALLY OPPRESSED!"

GET OUT.

#197 Auditions

#198 Fit to Print

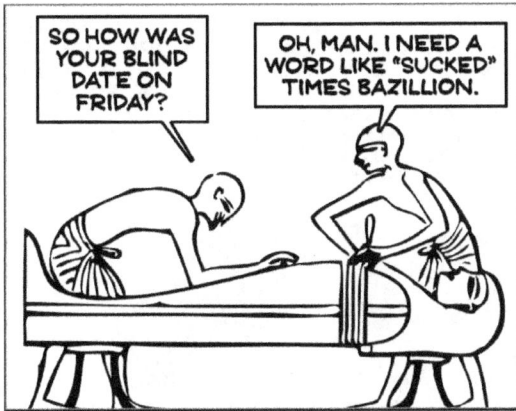

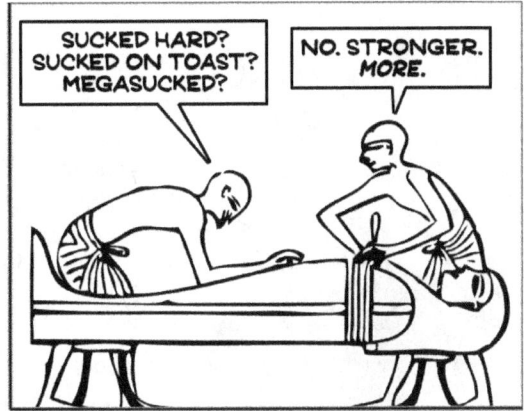

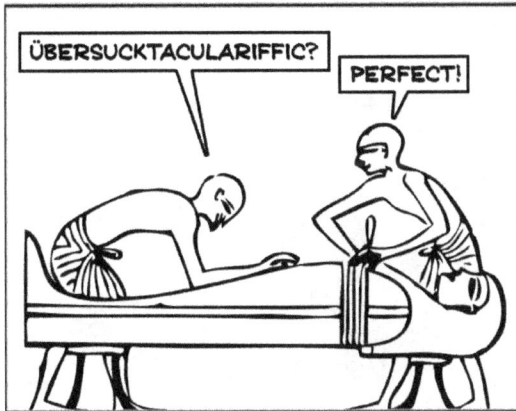

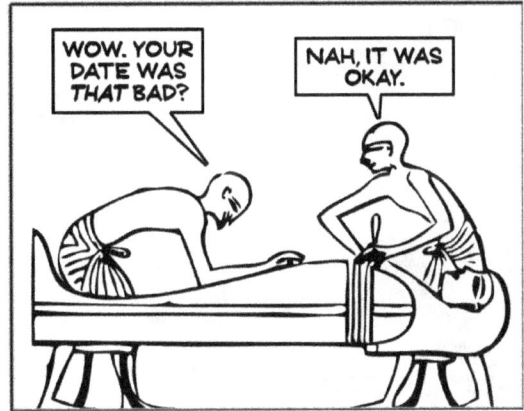

#199 Description

#200 Else What's a Heaven For?

#201 Q&A

#202 The Heart's Desire

#203 Lacunae

#204 Beverages

#205 With Apologies to Zhuangzi

#206 Rocks

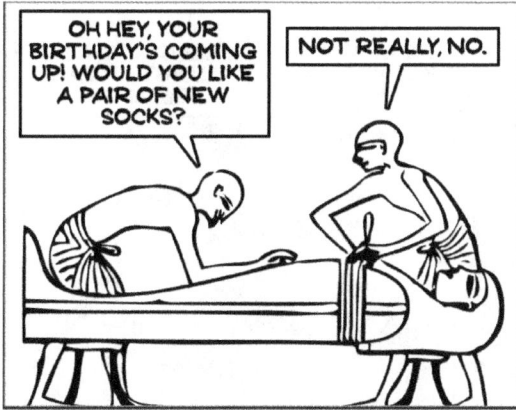

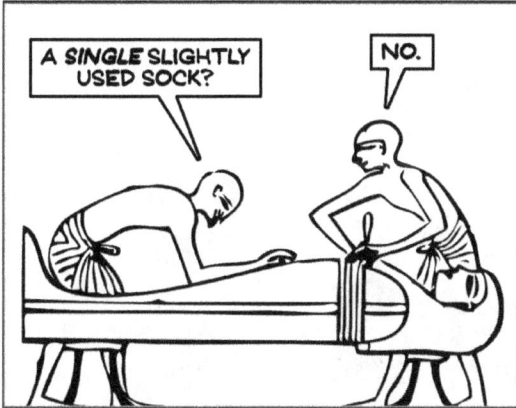

#207 Presents of Mind

#208 Late to the Meme

And still, at this late date, the variations are being promulgated! It's enough to make "I'M IN UR X, YING YOUR Z" look fresh and inventive.

#209 The Heart's Desire (a different one)

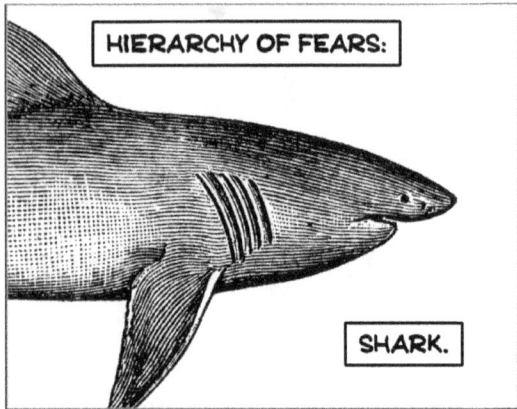

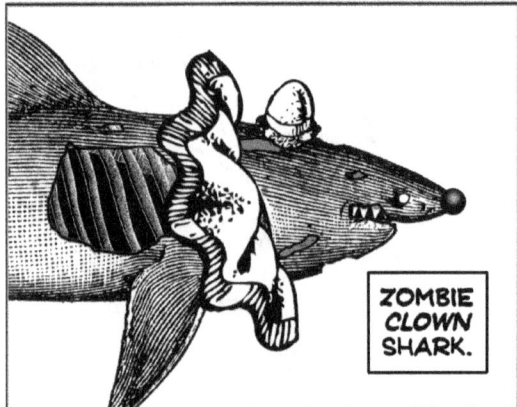

#210 Hierarchy of Fears

And yes, someone already quipped that the fourth panel is redundant of the third. (The main difference being that a shark doesn't keep track of his billable hours.)

#211 Halloween

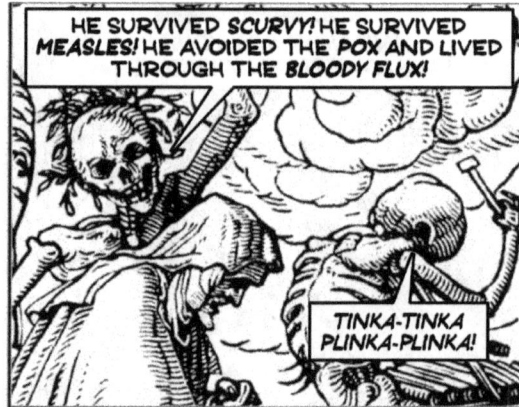

#212 Survivorship

#213 White House Dreams

#214 Social Niceties

#215 Behold the Power of Cheese

#216 River-Horse

#217 Holy Creepers

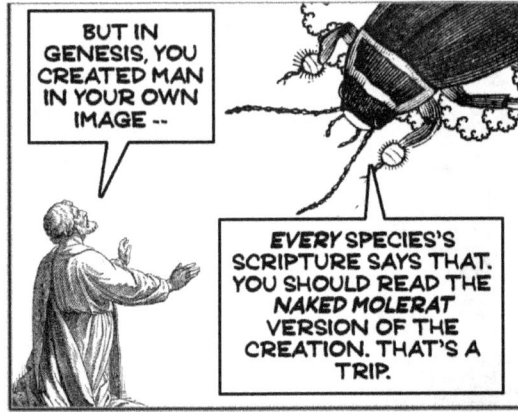

#218 Anthropomorphism Follies

#219 Divine Identity

Which is the point of the entire saga: Naps are awesome.

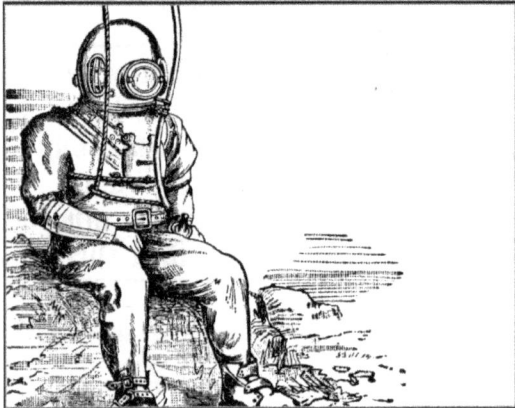

#220 Stop

#221 The Lone Syntactician

Doing this has always been my dream.

#222 Artistic Effects

This book is not responsible for any vapors gotten.

#223 Beyond Mere Mortals

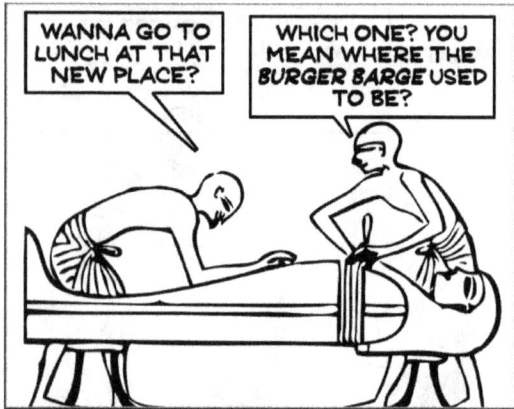

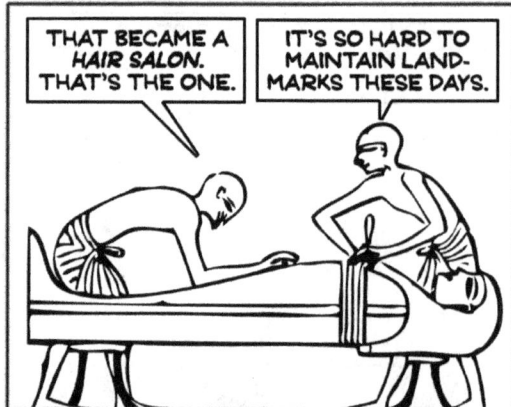

#224 The Palimpsest of Enterprise

#225 Holiday Preparations

EVERY CARTOONIST HAS EBBS AND FLOWS IN THE COMEDIC MUSE, AND WE HERE AT CHEAPCAFFEINE ARE NO DIFFERENT.

UNFORTUNATELY, AS THESE CARTOONS ARE USUALLY CREATED THE DAY THEY ARE POSTED, A LACK OF IMMEDIATE HUMOROUS INSPIRATION CAN BE A CRISIS.

IN SUCH SITUATIONS, MOST HUMORISTS HAVE STOCK GAGS UPON WHICH THEY CAN FALL BACK -- BOTH THOSE PARTICULAR TO THE VENUE, AND THOSE COMMON TO THE CULTURE.

ONE OF THE LATTER BEING THE WELL-PLACED FART JOKE.

PHOOT!

AND BY "WELL-PLACED," I MEAN "COMING OUT OF MY BUM."

#226 In Case of Emergency, Break Wind

#227 Holiday Prep

#228 The Hollyjollygeddon

#229 The Hollyjollygeddon Continues

That's right, I put Burl Ives's head on Jor Johnson's body.

#230 Hollyjollygeddon: The Final Chapter

Yup. I went there and stole a punchline from an image macro floating around the internet.

#231 Fishing For Ethics

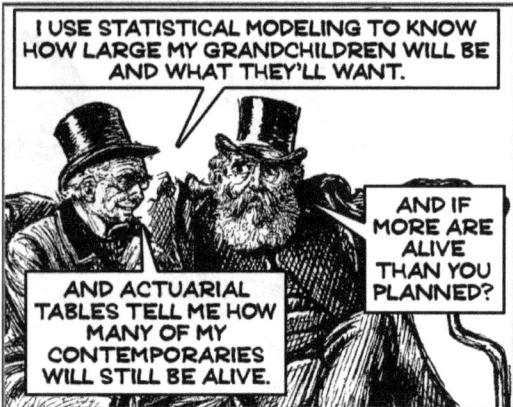

#232 Shopping By Numbers

#233 Be the Change

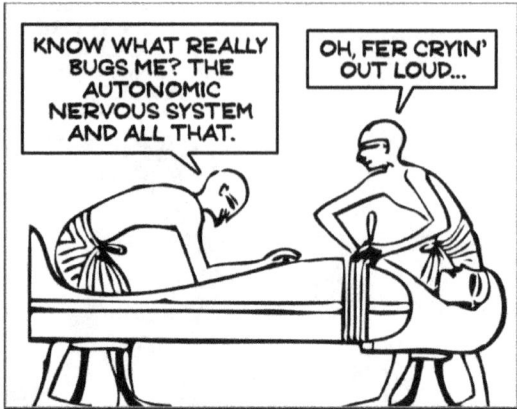

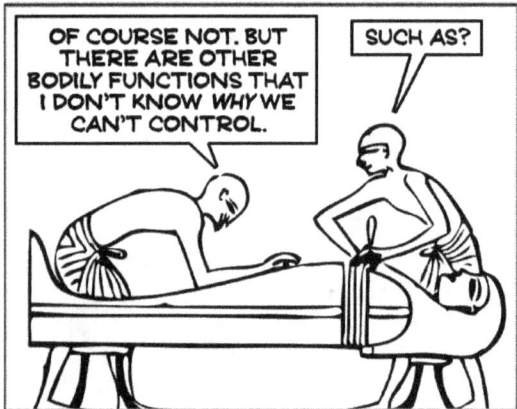

#234 Autonomy

#235 First Blood

#236 Procession

WE ARE VERY SORRY, BUT TODAY'S COMIC GOT LOST IN THE POST. PLEASE PRESENT YOUR RECEIPT AT THE SERVICE COUNTER FOR A FULL REFUND, AND BE SURE TO RETURN TOMORROW FOR ANOTHER INSTALLMENT.

"FART." THERE, ARE YOU HAPPY?

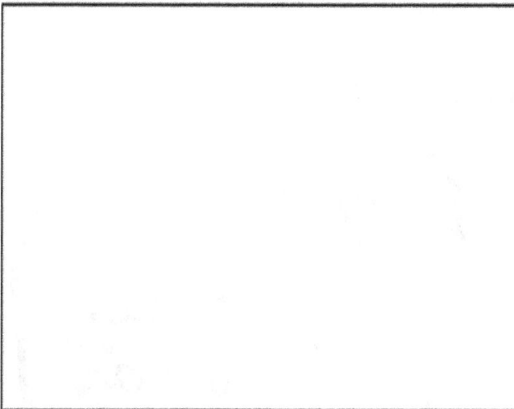

#237 Raincheck

Note: Due to a numbering error on my part, there is no comic #238.
   In its place, I present this original artwork: The HammerHydra! (SyFy Channel, you know where to reach me!)

Hammer-
Hydra

#239 Past Presents

#240 Drama, Unfortunately

You see, sometimes I work without a "buffer" of comics to post. So sometimes I just start in on situation and put words in the characters' mouths. And sometimes it doesn't turn out terribly funny, but I don't have time to start over and make a fresh comic before I've got to get out the door to my day job. So sometimes... this is what you get.

#241 Drama, Revisited

#242 Shopping

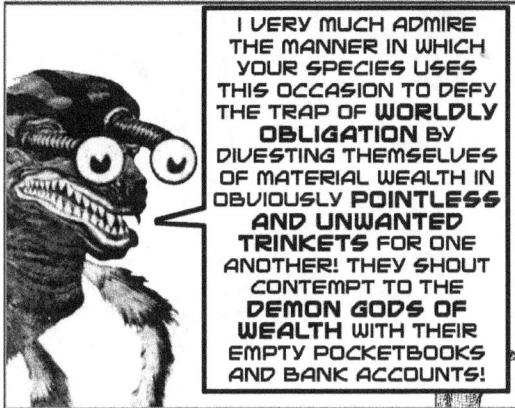

#243 'Tis the Season

#244 The Classics

CONFESSIONS AND REVELATIONS

I'VE NEVER READ *DUNE*.

I DON'T THINK SCARLETT JOHANSSON IS ALL THAT ATTRACTIVE.

I CAN NEVER REMEMBER WHO SINGS "MORE THAN A FEELING."

GEORGE BAILEY'S MELTDOWN IN *IT'S A WONDERFUL LIFE* ALWAYS MAKES ME CRY. SO DOES SPOCK'S DEATH IN *STAR TREK II*.

#245 Confessions and Revelations

All confessions are the cartoonist's own.

#246 Nobody Reads This, Right?

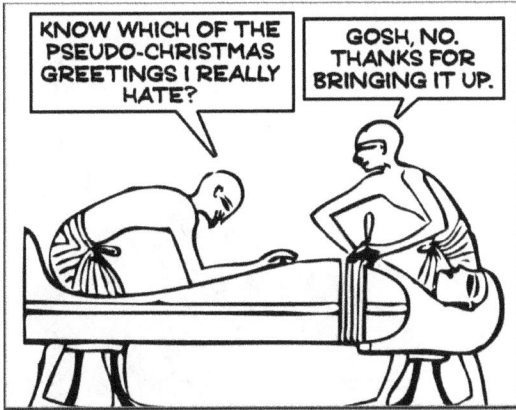

#247 Not That Season, the Other Season.

#248 Nobody's Even Reading These Over the Holidays, Right?

Of course, here in the book, I can't hide a comic like this during the week between Christmas and New Year's. I will therefore blame it on my evil twin.

#249 Let It Snow

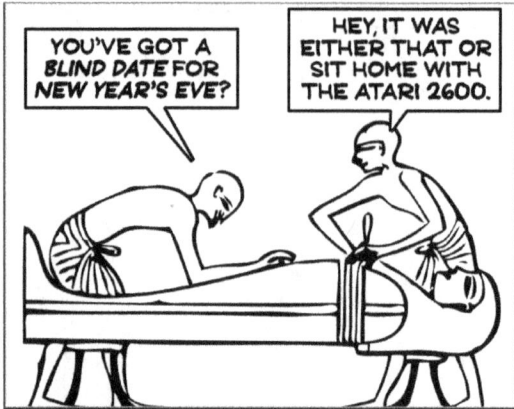

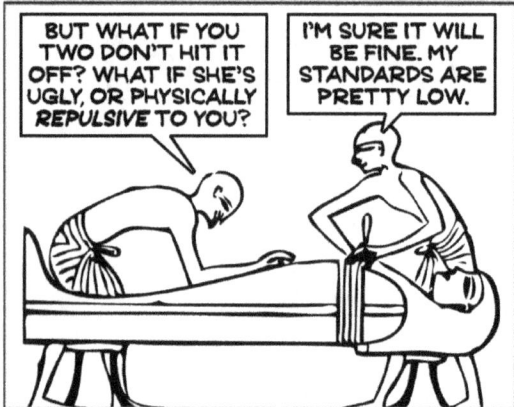

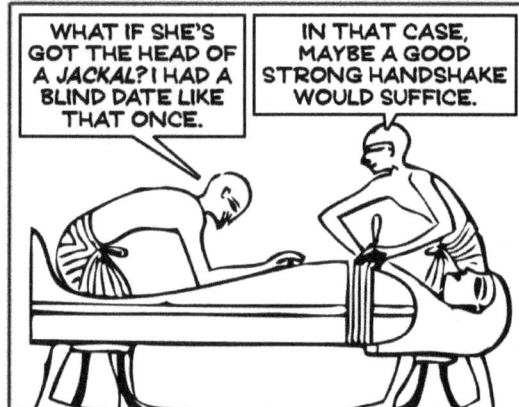

#250 Auld Acquaintance

#251 Resolutions

#252 Sic Transit

#253 Classics Afresh

#254 Correspondence

#255 Fifteen Minute Break

#256 Value

#257 Lyricism

#258 Stargazing

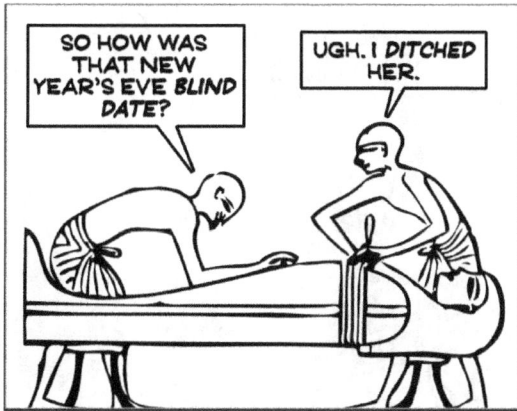

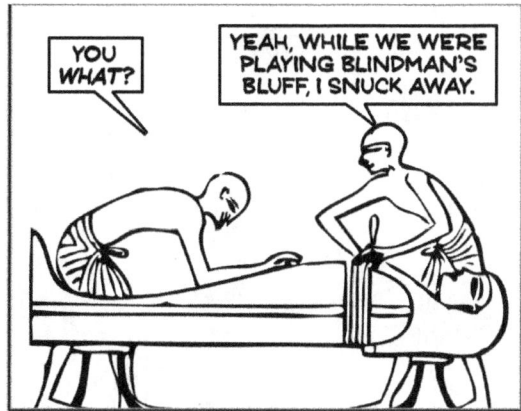

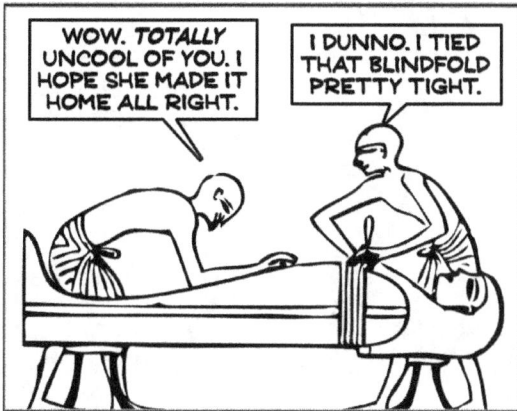

#259 Aftermath

#269 Giraffes

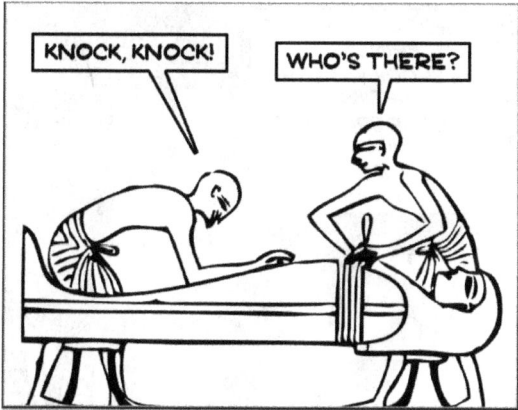

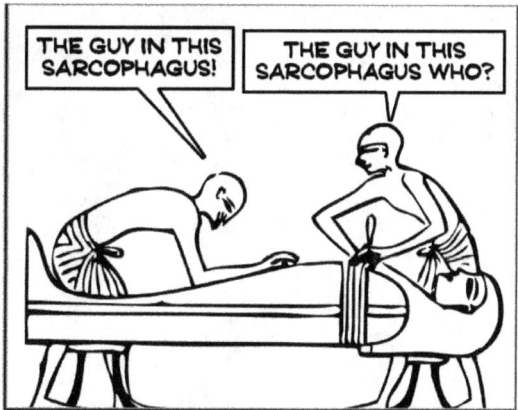

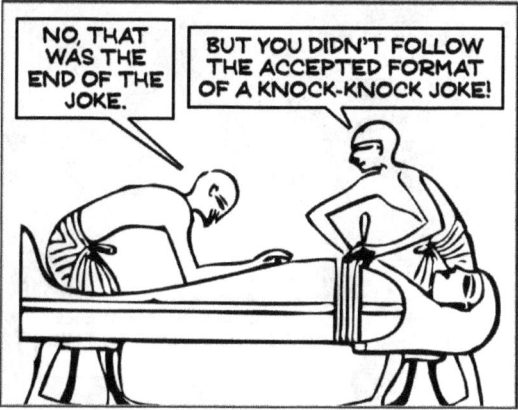

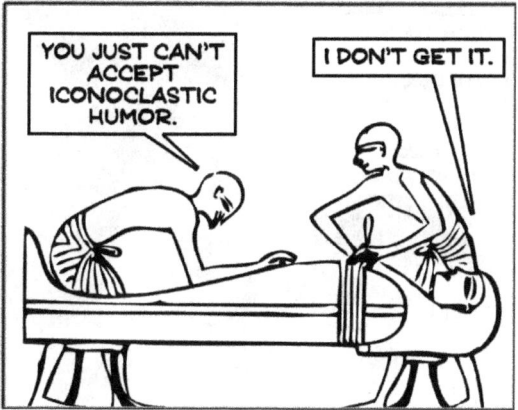

#261 Know Your Audience

#262 Second Verse, Same As the First

#263 Sacrifices Must Be Made

#264 Comedy is All About Setup

#265 The Glorious Future

Somehow it escaped me until after I had posted this comic that I had used for my punchline the running gag from *The Radio Adventures of Dr. Floyd*, an edutaining podcast about heroic time-travelers Dr. Floyd and his protégé Dr. Grant preventing evil time-traveler Dr. Steve from stealing artifacts of historical significance he can then sell on Ebay. Check it out at *doctorfloyd.com*.

#266 Timelessness is Hard

#267 Elephantine Concerns

#268 The Cuisine of the Other

#269 The Final Ethnocentric Frontier

#270 Staticism

And the kicker is that there *were* no such complaints. I waited and waited for one so I'd have an excuse for this joke, but when no such criticism was forthcoming, I took matters into my own hands.

#271 Vote With Your Feet

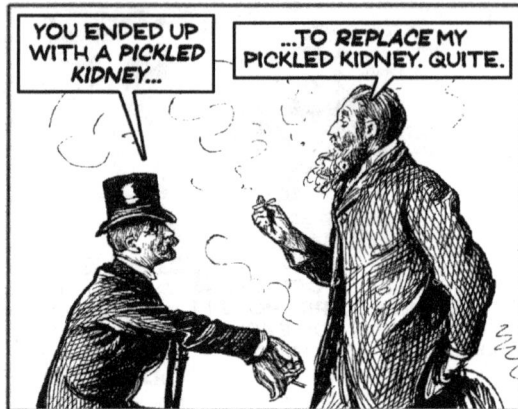

#272 Of Kidneys

#273 Barely Autobiographical At All

#274 Amusements

#275 Seasons

HI, THERE. I'M *THE SUN*. YOU MAY HAVE SEEN ME BEFORE -- LIKE, ALMOST *EVERY DAY* OF YOUR LIFE, UNLESS YOU LIVE IN SEATTLE.

MOST PEOPLE ONLY THINK OF ME AS A HUGE, REMOTE BALL OF FUSION, BUT I'M NOT *JUST* THAT. I HAVE *FEELINGS* TOO.

MM-HMM. THAT'S RIGHT. KIND OF MAKES YOU STOP AND THINK, DOESN'T IT?

GRANTED, MOST OF MY FEELINGS ARE *"HOTHOTHOTHOTHOTHOTHOT,"* BUT THEY'RE STILL FEELINGS.

#276 You Are My Sunshine

#277 A Hard Day's Half-Century

#278 Magic

#279 Contentment

#280 The Essence of Fishness

#281 Safety First

#282 Valentine Observance

#283 Safety

#284 The Long Tail

ERRATUM: IN A PREVIOUS COMIC, THE ROCKS PICTURED BELOW WERE LABELED AS "FUNNY ROCKS."

UPON FURTHER EXAMINATION, WE HAVE CONCLUDED THAT THESE PARTICULAR ROCKS EXHIBIT NO HUMOROUS, COMEDIC OR RISIBLE QUALITIES.

IT WAS NOT THE INTENT OF CHEAPCAFFEINE TO PERPETRATE SUCH A MISCHARACTERIZATION UPON THE READING PUBLIC. WE SINCERELY REGRET THE ERROR.

THIS GUY, HOWEVER, IS FREAKIN' HILARIOUS.
-THE MANAGEMENT

#285 Erratum

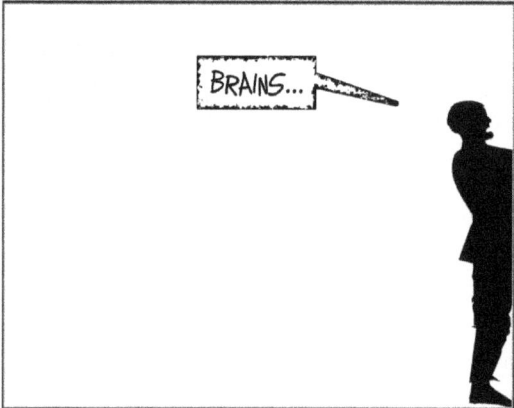

#286 Brains, As Noted

#287 Names By the Pound

#288 Rules

#289 Of Bovine Bondage

That's right, a lazy punchline.

#290 Doors

#291 Vita-Life

#292 The Spaceman's Chorus

In case you're wondering, these lyrics were composed to the chorus tune from the Bugs Bunny cartoon "What's Up, Doc?" (1950).

IT'S TIME FOR MASHUPS!

MICROSOFT  GOOGLE

MICROOGLE

THE CHURCH OF JESUS CHRIST OF LATTER-DAY SAINTS  REV. SUN MYUNG MOON'S UNIFICATION CHURCH

MORMOONIES

THE WANDERING JEW  THE FLYING DUTCHMAN

THE MEANDERING DUTCH JEW

ISLAMIC JIHADISTS  WESTBORO BAPTIST CHURCH

A SLIGHTLY LESS ANNOYING WESTBORO BAPTIST CHURCH

#293 Mashups

#294 It's All About Recruitment

#295 Procession

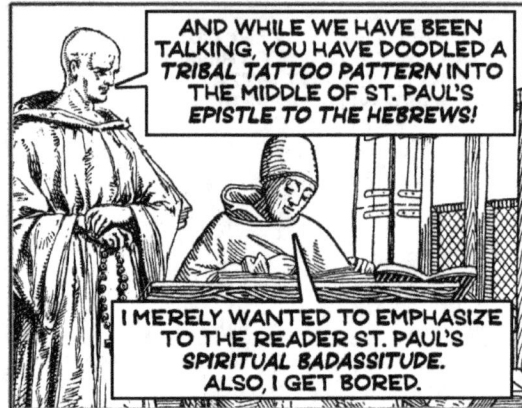

#296 Illumination

#297 Ultra-Illumination

#298 Quandaries

#299 Temptations

#300 Temptation Triumphant

The Adventure Continues at

www.CheapCaffeine.net

www.ingramcontent.com/pod-product-compliance
Lightning Source LLC
Chambersburg PA
CBHW080659110426
42739CB00034B/3332